HOW TO MAKE MONEY WITH CLICKBANK

THE FASTEST AND EASIEST WAY TO MAKE MONEY ONLINE

MICHAEL GREENE

CONTENTS

INTRODUCTION

This book is designed to be simple and easy to read so that even the newbie Internet marketer will have no problem understanding it. It contains proven steps and strategies on how to consistently and easily make money online using Clickbank. You'll learn how to be one of the 5% of people who are making tens of thousands of dollars a month online by following these strategies I'm about to introduce to you.

I will take you step-by-step and show you what to do to begin making money online. All you have to do is follow the steps in this book and you'll be on your way to making a passive income online. However, I must mention this is *not* a get-rich-quick-scheme. This will take effort and time and if you are willing to put that in, I guarantee you will be reap the rewards.

The best part is that this book will save you so much time and energy because you will skip over much of the years of trial and error I put into figuring out how to make money with Clickbank.

Now, if you're ready, we can begin with the first step –
figuring out why you should choose to market products from
Clickbank.

THE WHAT & THE WHY OF CLICKBANK

Affiliate Marketing is the most common way to make a lot of money online. Essentially what you're doing is promoting other people's' products and earning a commission. If you're new to online marketing and making money on the Internet, one of the first names that will become familiar to you is ClickBank. You probably have seen videos of people making tons of money through that strange thing called affiliate marketing. Some of the videos out there may seem too far fetched or just too good to be true. One of the most common affiliate marketing outfits you will find out there is ClickBank. It has been hailed as one of the best affiliate marketing portals for many years.

ClickBank has been around since 1998 and has over 10,000 digital product vendors who have designed products to be marketed and sold online. Usually the products can be downloaded right then and there either using a download link, or accessing a password protected website. Clickbank has made over $2.5 billion in sales.

The results and the efforts put in by different affiliate marketing entrepreneurs differ one from another. Some have been moderately successful and making sustainable income on the side. Some have made some pretty decent money that allowed them to do this full time. Some have even made six figure incomes. This site has allowed thousands of online marketers to earn a full time living and generated most of the income passively.

The Risk of Failure

But being bluntly honest about it, there are those who eventually failed. Frankly speaking, affiliate marketing is a business. That is also very true of every form of Internet marketing for that matter. Just so you know, remember that every business enterprise also incurs a certain degree of risk. Even the most successful online marketers have received a certain degree of failure – especially those who have made six figure incomes.

However, as you may have heard a thousand times before – fortune favors the bold. Only those who take the risk are truly worthy of great returns. Note that with great risk come great rewards. Every mistake and failure you make should only waft you ever closer to the level of success that everyone aspires for.

So Why Stick with ClickBank?

There are a lot of reasons to patronize ClickBank's affiliate program. Take note that this company was hailed as the leading affiliate network back in 2011. That alone speaks volumes about the things they have to offer. It's also proof of how great their system is and how relevant the products are that they advertise. Besides, the company's track record sort of gives them a lot of bragging rights in the world of Internet marketing.

You can look at the company as a huge marketplace where product makers and promoters can make a good deal of money. It's a market portal where electronic goods are put on display and sold. Note that the products you have to market are not necessarily tangible. Some of them are software applications, eBooks, and just about anything that you can download onto your computer.

The company's database contains literally thousands of digital products. Online publishers come to ClickBank so that people like you and me can market and sell their products and make a profit as well in return. It's a Win/Win solution for both the publisher and the affiliate marketer.

WHAT WORKS AND WHAT DOESN'T

As mentioned earlier, not everyone who signs up for an account in ClickBank makes money out of the endeavor. Some, at the very least make sporadic earnings. They may make some money now, then they stop for a short season, and then they try it all over again. That might work but it's not going to be that lucrative to make you want to quit your day job.

NOW, you might be wondering why there is a large discrepancy in the results. Everyone knows that the Click-Bank affiliate program works. It definitely makes money— no question about it. The difference of course lies in the approach people use to market the hundreds of download-able digital products available.

NEWBIE ERRORS

There are online marketing entrepreneurs that sign up for a ClickBank account, make Squidoo lenses, Hubpages hubs, blogs, or write an article for EzineArticles, place their hop links and think that that's it. Sometimes it works and sometimes it doesn't. To be honest, that's only one small fraction of what an online marketer should do to make good money through this enterprise.

ANOTHER COMMON IDEA that comes to the minds of some affiliate marketers follows this pattern...First, they choose a product in the ClickBank database. They create a landing page for the said products that they want to promote. Then they send traffic to the said pages using pay per click(PPC) and pay per view (PPV) advertising. And finally, they make some profit.

THERE ARE newbie marketers who think that way especially if they have cash to burn. It may work but it will come at a cost. Remember that using the marketing strategy mentioned, you will be spending a good deal of money paying for PPC/PPV services just to drive traffic to your site or landing page.

NOT EVERYONE HAS cash to burn and the above-mentioned marketing scheme will not work for people who have limited funds. You can end up spending $2,000 for traffic generating service and all the other costs involved and earn $4,000 in the effort. Add to that the risk that the traffic generation campaign may fail at a certain point then you can be investing a lot of money and end up losing a huge portion of your investment.

.   .   .

STATISTICS ALSO SHOW that using the above mentioned method of spending a good amount of money to drive traffic to your site is not a stable way to get people to visit your page or portal. In effect, you are spending a lot of money just to get one person to actually purchase the items you have advertised. In short, the above method is not cost effective and it also runs the risk of running your business in the ground.

GOING BACK **to Business Basics**

IN ORDER TO make your online endeavor a profitable one, you really need to get back to some business basics. It's a scratch my back and I'll scratch yours world out there. This means that you will only get good business if you make good rapport with your target market. In other words, there is a lot of money to be made establishing a relationship with your customers and making them repeat customers. Eventually, that's **how to really make money with ClickBank**.

THE BUSINESS OF MAKING MONEY WITH CLICKBANK

Let's face the facts. There are Internet marketers who think that they are just playing a game. Some even think that it's a get rich quickly sort of business. If it were anything of the sort then you should have seen hundreds if not thousands of people who have made more than six figure incomes via the online marketing.

IN REALITY, making money with ClickBank or with any affiliate marketing outfit will really take a lot of hard work. Do you want to know why? The reason is simple – it's a business. You're not playing in the virtual world, although it may feel like it at times. You're actually trying to deal with people, although you don't really get to meet them in person.

REMEMBER that the subject of money is a very emotional subject. A lot of emotions come into play before people will be willing enough to part with their hard earned cash. Trust must be built between the customers and the business entity that they are transacting with.

YOU CAN LOOK at it like coffee shop. You can find dozens of coffee shops nowadays but why do you think some folks keep coming back to their own preferred places for coffee? The answer is simple, they love the coffee, they love the ambiance, they love the service, and they love the entire business package.

YOU SHOULD LOOK at your online business enterprise in the same light if you really want to master **how to make money with ClickBank**. You need to differentiate your business now that you have spotted an opportunity that you can capitalize on.

YOU ALSO NEED to establish a working relationship with your customers. Remember that there is greater potential for profit out of ten repeat visitors than 50 one-time visitors that will never come back. The ten repeat visitors that you get will eventually buy one product. After that, if they have a good experience with the product that they purchased then, they are more likely to come back and buy something else. They will eventually be willing to recommend your online business and spread the word with trust already established.

REMEMBER that if you offer nothing of value to your customers then they will likely never come back. When you design your online marketing campaigns, make sure that you give your visitors something that they can take home with them that will enrich their lives. You then are proverbially scratching their backs and eventually they will scratch yours. And hopefully they will come back once more to keep scratching your back until your itch is satisfied – metaphorically speaking.

SELECTING YOUR NICHE

Early on, we mentioned that you need to differentiate your business on the Internet. Other than that, we should also talk about something that is related to that very subject – segmentation. Other than just making a different brand or packaging your ClickBank products in a totally new way, you should also identify a specific market segment where you can work well with and eventually make money from.

THE SCIENCE **of Segmentation and Differentiation**

Differentiation refers to making your business unique to the eyes of visitors. In other words, you should be showing customers something that they haven't seen before. Eventually this differentiation will be their reason for coming back. Remember that you're not the first one to market ClickBank products. So why should visitors choose you over the hundreds of others out there?

Try to answer that question and if you can find it then you're one step closer to making eventual success. If you give them a reason to come back (and if they do like the way you present your stuff) then they will become repeat customers. Remember that people don't like being sold to. The first thing in the minds of the ordinary consumer is what is in it for me. They want to know what unique valuable thing it is that you can give to them.

Zeroing in on Your Niche

Eternally related to differentiating yourself from the competition is segmentation. You cannot completely differentiate your business without first identifying your market segment. In the language of Internet marketing, that translates to finding your specific niche.

Remember that there may be hundreds of products on ClickBank to promote but you must identify a specific niche of products that work together. For instance, you don't want to sell a graphically intense multiplayer online game along with corporate software all in the same site or page.

Every entrepreneur must know that a well-diversified or differentiated business that serves a very specific segment of the market (i.e. a very specific niche) is more likely to succeed in the long run compared to a business that tries to serve everything to everybody. Identifying your market segment and differentiating your business accordingly gives your business a degree of character, which later on becomes something that your particular business becomes known for.

So, next time you visit the pages of ClickBank, find a set of products that are related that also serve a particular niche. Find keywords that you can use that are related to those products as well as key search terms that people actually use when they look for similar products that you intend to market.

To Do:

1. Choose A Specific Niche (e.g. Relationships, Health, or Vegetarian Diets) – and choose a niche you like to keep your interest and motivation up. After you've selected a niche, go ahead and select a popular product in your niche.

2. Choose A Product As soon as you create a Clickbank account you can look through Clickbank Marketplace to determine which products fit in your niche. Most of the products are e-books, video, and audio files. The first products listed are the most popular- by default. It will also tell you how much you will make for each sale, and the average rebill total if it's a recurring sale. In addition you can view the gravity, which is very important. The higher the gravity number, the more popular the product – hence, the more sales it's making. A low gravity number means (such as below 5) that the product isn't very popular and people aren't promoting it – this is usually because it's not a good product. Therefore, when choosing a product to sell, you'll want to lean towards products with a higher gravity.

Go ahead and check out a few of the websites listed to see if one of the products catches your eye. Once you've chosen a product, you'll want to check its credibility, reliability, and quality. This is where customer reviews can come in handy. So go ahead and Google search for customer reviews of your product.

Casting Your Line with a Lure

It's interesting that before you can sell something to people you must first give them something for free. One good strategy that is used by some food stores (or any new business establishments) is that they give away free samples of their products. It actually does two things: (1) it advertises and spreads word about the new establishment; and (2) the free gift is a way to lure potential customers into the store.

Translating That Concept in ClickBank Marketing

Now how do you translate that concept in terms of online marketing? Here's **how to make money with ClickBank** using that very concept. The idea is to give them something that they will perceive as valuable or something that is actually valuable to them. The free gift is declared free but it actually is traded for something – your prospect's email address. It's actually a fair trade come to think of it. Both parties get something that is valuable to them.

There was an online marketer who raffled off iPads to prospective customers in exchange for their emails and referrals. He was able to gather thousands of emails in the process. Guess what, other marketers followed suit trying to mimic the strategy and also trying to obtain the same level of success.

You don't really have to spend a lot of money just to give away something for free that can be valuable to your prospective clients. But if you have the funds to give away then by all means give away free iPads.

There is another alternative that other marketers use which is not as expensive. That is by giving away a free eBook. An eBook, a free one at that, is also perceived as equally important or just valuable as any high tech gizmo on the planet. Information is usually a prized possession especially in the Information Age.

The eBook that you will be giving away for free will be talking about your selected niche. You may include some of the products that you are marketing in the eBook. For instance, if you're selected niche is about MMORPG games and tutorials then you can advertise some games in the book and direct some traffic to your site or directly to a sales page.

Take note that you don't have to write the eBook yourself. You can hire a ghostwriter to write the eBook for you. It will save you the time and effort. Hiring virtual assistant writer to make you an eBook will allow you to focus your energies on more important matters. The important thing is that you leave precise instructions for your writer to follow.

Note that your free eBook doesn't have to be 100 pages long. It can be as short as 20 pages or as much as 50 to 60 pages long. Anything longer will be too costly for you or just too time consuming. The important thing is that the book should cover exactly the niche of ClickBank products that you intend to market.

Remember that the information in your eBook should be worth the information that your prospects are giving you. They are allowing you to talk to them even further down the line and perhaps convert page visit to actual sales in the near future. If you intend to write the eBook yourself, make sure you cover enough about the niche that brings the reader value.

Creating a Squeeze Page to Build an Email List

You don't have to dedicate an entire website to gather prospective client emails. You can create a one page squeeze page or landing page. The main idea behind a squeeze page is to make your eBook convincing enough so that its visitors will be willing enough to give you their email addresses.

The emails that you gather from the squeeze page will be added to your email list. The conversion rate of these opt in pages will vary greatly. Some of these landing pages convert as few as five percent of its visitors. On the other hand, there are squeeze pages that convert up to 60% of its visitors.

Remember that the goal here is not to sell anything. The goal is to make your page's visitors provide you with the key to reach them in the future. Call it a Trojan horse but hey, you're giving away something that your prospects can actually use. In that regard, this marketing tool is neither deceptive nor abusive in nature since it is mutually beneficial.

To Do:

1. **Create an Ebook for your niche** that you can offer for free to anyone who subscribe to your email/article list. It is common to use http://ezinearticles.com to submit your articles and build credibility, bringing more traffic to your website.

2. **Create a landing page** that sends them to a page (these are called Squeeze pages), where they can enter their email address and become potential subscribers to your articles. Then, use autoresponders to send the articles out

It's important to develop a "landing page" that introduces the product to the customer. You can have them created for dirt cheap at www.fiverr.com. Another note, is to keep the words on your landing page to a minimum because often on landing pages, there are too many words and the reader feels overwhelmed and loses interest. So, just write about the top 5 features about the product. And make sure to have a link to the sales page where they can purchase the product. This may sound confusing right now, but once you start doing it and implementing what you're learning, you'll catch on quickly.

Once that's completed, you can go back to Clickbank

and obtain the affiliate link to promote the product and post it. Then you can sell it and begin making money. As soon as you make a sale, you will be making a passive income – the tricky part is to keep generating traffic to your affiliate link or website.

DRIVING THE TRAFFIC HOME

There are two ways to drive traffic and let people click the affiliate links you posted and eventually earn your commissions. The first way to do it is by getting generic searches from online search engines. The second one is the method we described earlier where you build your market base by gathering emails and making mailing lists where you can directly contact possible clients.

Both methods work. However, many experts and big names in online marketing have said time and again that the money is in the mailing list. Affiliate marketing A-list folks like Shoemoney (he launched what is known in ClickBank as the Shoemoney System), John Reese, John Chow, and also Frank Kern have used and continue to use mailing lists. That is one of their secrets on how to make money with ClickBank.

When you depend on generic searches from search engines you basically create pages and use search engine optimization to your advantage. It's like casting your lines into the water with the bait in it. You end up waiting for the fish to come to you and eventually take a bite. The mailing list approach sort of spins things around because you are the one who comes to the market and tries to lure the fish closer until you eventually catch one.

You can try either one or you can try both. However, experience has shown that the more experienced and successful online marketers definitely build their customer base along with their mailing list. The main advantage of a mailing list is that you already have a captive audience.

One way or another they somehow, to certain degree, know your brand and have trust in your business (even though at times there is just a little amount of trust in there). You have already proven your usefulness, provided that the free eBook you gave was really useful to them. If they like your eBook then they will enjoy the stuff you say in your mails. That will eventually lead to conversion which means you get an eventual sale.

Building Your Mailing List

As mentioned earlier, one of the time tested tools to gather the emails of prospective clients and repeat customers is by making a squeeze page and offering your free eBook there in exchange for their email addresses. The fastest way to drive traffic into your squeeze page is nothing more than paid advertising. In the world of Internet marketing, it means that you will pay for pay per click (PPC) and pay per view (PPV) advertising.

There are lots of outfits that offer these services. But finding them is the least of your worries. Like we mentioned earlier, PPC and PPV are the most expensive ways to drive traffic to your site or page. They are effective, yes, but there is a limit to that. You can see it as a well. One day it will dry up. It will work for a time letting you reel in decent amounts (sometimes really big amounts) of money.

Freebies To Give Away in Exchange for Email Addresses

There are other ways to getting traffic to your site and there are things that you can give away to make people want to trade their email addresses with you. Some experts at certain fields offer free passes to their webinars where they talk about topics that fall within their respective fields of study (aka their niche).

The webinars are free but the attendees are required to sign up for their mailing list. That means they visit the squeeze page or landing page you made and leave their email addresses at the door. Webinars also allow you to interact directly (live!) with your prospective clients. They can immediately tell through this experience if you are really worth their time and money.

Now, you don't have to be the expert that does the talking during these webinars. You can actually hire one for a fee. If it works, that one-time fee you pay the expert to spill the beans in your selected niche will pay off several times in the future since you can use the email addresses that you have gathered in different online marketing campaigns. There is more than one way to milk the cow, metaphorically speaking.

Other than eBooks and webinars, there are other things that you can offer that will be of value to your prospective repeat customers. If your niche is about music then you can give away free music. For instance, if your market segment is about people who are new to guitar playing then you can send short training videos on guitar playing basics.

Within the short training video you can offer even more intense training material that they will have to pay for of course. But the initial training video will be free and all they need to part with in the process is their email addresses. If training videos aren't your thing or you're slightly camera shy then you can just make an audiobook and give it away. If your voice sounds not very appealing then hire someone to read your material and record it.

The important thing is that you are able to think out of the box and give something away that contains material related to your niche.

Build Your Customer Relationship

You can call this the secret ingredient of the secret sauce of every successful person who has learned **how to make money with ClickBank** or any other online marketing outfit. You see, some people have built lists of up to 40,000 email addresses and still make small profit. There are online marketers who are only able to build shorter email address lists, perhaps just around 10,000 email addresses, and make six figure sales.

The big difference is that the successful ones are those who are able to build their relationship with their customers. This is why it has been stated in the beginning of this book that you should never underestimate the value of a repeat customer.

The first step to do this is to build your relationship with the people who subscribed to you (i.e. the people who traded their email addresses for the eBook or any other freebie that you gave away). You already have their email addresses and it's now time to put that into use.

Using Auto Responders

One of the tools of the trade is using auto responders. These are emails that are sent out at different dates and at different intervals. These auto responders help to build that subtle relationship with your prospective clients. Other than that, they are also promotional materials that remind your customer base about your blog or squeeze page or website.

Other than promoting your particular brand, they are also marketing tools that can be used to market the Click-Bank products in your niche that may help cover their needs or solve their problems. I suggest that you send these promotional emails some time later. The first emails should be the ones that build rapport with your customer base.

Remember that customers don't always buy things during their first visit to your squeeze page or even in the first email that you sent them. Continue to give your prospects things that will be valuable to them through your emails. This means that you don't throw in your sales pitch at the start. Do that later when they have learned to trust you and your brand.

Now, crafting these emails is a work of art in itself. They are also one of those tools that have a double edge. It can make or break your customer base. So, I suggest that if you lack the skills to write crafty emails then hire someone to write them for you. It may cost you some money but you will get a lot in return.

One important reminder here is that you should also allow the people in your list to opt out of the program. This means that if they want to get their email address off your list then allow them to do so. This will help you to keep only customers to your target market in your database.

To Do:

1. **Write Articles or blogs** and put a link to your affiliate product in each article. This will lead people who search for a particular product on a search engine to your product page, and they may purchase your product through this link - just obtain the affiliate link to promote the product. On average, it is recommended to write around 40 arti-

cles a month, and make sure to include your landing page in each article. They can be short and too the point, with the primary purpose being to generate traffic. Put your subscribers on your autoresponder so that they will get an email every time you post a new article. This is a great way to keep a consistent base of customers and generate consistent sales.

2. **Learn SEO.** In order to be extremely successful with Clickbank you will need to learn how to do SEO (Search Engine Optimization) to get your blog and/or website to rank high on search engines. This will bring in more traffic hence more potential customers who'll click on your landing page.

3. **Promote your blog, website, and affiliate product on Social Media sites.** You can begin groups in Facebook that are related to your niche to build a targeted potential customer base. You can also use sites such as Twitter.com, and LinkedIn to promote your affiliate products.

Additional Recommendations:

1. **Get a coach or mentor.** Naturally you will have questions about what to do when affiliate marketing and using Clickbank. An experienced coach who has had success with affiliate marketing can save you a lot of time and stress.

2. **Make sure you have a set schedule to work** (for example 10am-1pm and 3pm to 8pm) with no distractions. When working from home it is too easy to get distracted by external things, such as TV, Facebook, checking emails, phone calls, etc., so stick to a schedule.

AFTERWORD

While some people have immediate success with Clickbank and affiliate marketing, for most people it takes at least a few months because you need to build the relationships with potential customers. Again, this is due to the fact that it may take a few months to build up your article subscriber/email list according to your niche. Of course, if you already have a large subscriber/email list this process will be shorter. Therefore you may have to be patient, and persistent before bringing in the big bucks.

Thank you and I wish you the best of luck!